BE A SUPER AWESOME ARTIST

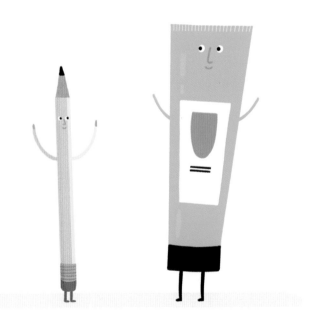

Henry Carroll & Rose Blake

Laurence King Publishing

Contents

So you want to be a super-awesome artist?

Well, you've come to the right place because this book will have you painting like Pollock, doodling like Duchamp and creating like Kahlo in no time. Don't know who they are? You will soon!

Inside you'll find works of art by the world's most super-awesome artists, who often act crazier than kids. All you need to do is look at the artworks, read a little about what makes them so great and then channel the artistic genius within to make your own mega-masterpieces. Along the way

you'll also be introduced to some all-important "Nifty know-hows" that will help you on your quest to achieving artistic excellence.

To complete these challenges, you'll need to arm yourself with some essential tools. The ones that super-awesome artists use every day. These include graphite pencils, coloured pencils, an eraser, a sharpener, brushes, acrylic paints, scissors, glue, a camera phone, card and paper – lots and lots of lovely paper in all different colours. Now turn the page and let's get creating!

Challenge yourself
Look out for this icon if you need extra inspiration to complete a challenge.

#BeSuperAwesome
Use this hashtag to share your own super-awesome artworks and take a peek at everyone else's.

Stay in line

Let's ease you in to becoming a super-awesome artist with a challenge inspired by one of the most famous artists of all, Mr Pablo Picasso. Although Pablo used only one continuous line for this drawing, we instantly know it's a dog. Not just that, it's a sausage dog. Pablo makes it look easy, but it actually takes some serious skills to capture the essence of a subject using just one line. The trick is to focus on the main features – in this case, the dog's snout, ears, legs, long body and tail. Use one continuous line to make your own characterful drawings of animals.

Have fun drawing your animals. Exaggerate some of the features to inject a bit of humour. Don't worry too much about them looking realistic.

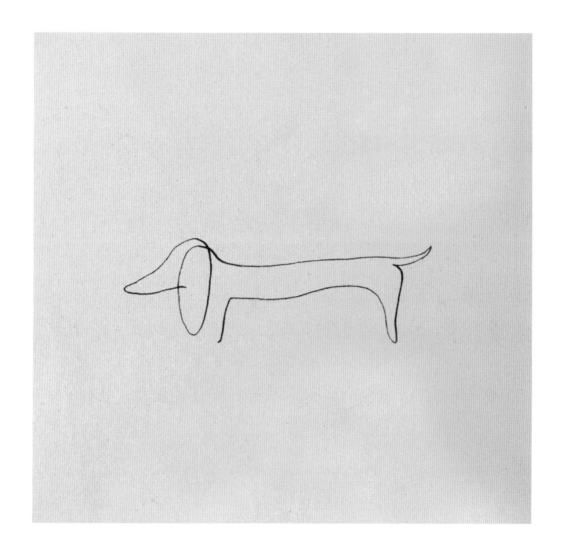

Pablo Picasso, 'Dachshund/Sausage Dog', detail in pen and Indian
ink on beige paper from a sketchbook Zervos VI n°972 (1907)

Jackson Pollock, *Convergence* (1952)

Be a drip

This guy called Jackson Pollock made super-awesome paintings without even touching the canvas. Jackson would dip his brushes in pots of paint and then drip the paint all over his canvas, which was laid out on the floor. The paintings would take on a life of their own as he flicked and dripped different colours, making them more and more layered. The results were a tangle of lines that reflect Jackson's movements as he made the painting. Although he didn't have total control of the marks, it's amazing how precise this composition looks. It goes without saying what this challenge is... Let's get dripping!

Start by laying out your paper on the living room carpet. ONLY KIDDING! PLEASE DON'T DO THAT! This challenge is going to get messy, so it is best done outside. Before you start, think about the order in which you want to drip the colours because this is all about creating layers of lines. Oh, and acrylic paints will work best for this.

Have fun with faces

Lorna Simpson is a super-awesome artist who made artworks using cut-outs from *Ebony*, a magazine for African-American readers. After a while, all the models in magazines kind of look the same because that's just how models tend to look. So Lorna decided to cut out the faces of models and then paint amazing hairstyles on them. Rather than look "generic", the faces in Lorna's pictures become a celebration of individuality, colour and joy! Cut out the faces you find in magazines and then think of creative ways to bring them to life.

You could paint hair on your cut-out faces, like Lorna, or give them crazy accessories, like hats, earrings and glasses. However you choose to transform them, make sure you leave enough space to paint around your heads when you position them on the paper.

Lorna Simpson, Selection of *Ebony Collages* (2011–12)

Bridget Riley, *Straight Curve* (1963)

Go with the flow

I love Bridget Riley's paintings, mainly because I get to use one of my favourite words – "discombobulated". It means feeling a bit dizzy or confused, which is how I feel when I look at Bridget's painting. She only used black and white triangles, but see how crazy her creation is to look at. Even though it just contains straight lines, everything seems so curvy and appears to move like waves in the ocean. It's amazing how a flat picture can become so three-dimensional to the point of being almost impossible to look at! Try making your own pattern painting or drawing that creates a similar effect.

If you look closely at Bridget's painting, you'll see that it's basically a grid, but she's gradually changed the size and shape of each square to create lines that appear to "flow". Perhaps start by shading squares on gridded paper in slightly different ways, and then have a go at creating your own grids.

Get grubby

Artists like Andy Goldsworthy make their artworks outside, using natural materials such as leaves, sticks, stones, snow and ice. Believe it or not, Andy made this piece by arranging autumn leaves of different colours. Normally artists want their work to last forever, but what's so super-awesome about Andy's art is that before long it collapses, melts or gets blown or washed away. There's something beautiful about knowing your creation will exist for only a few fleeting hours, days or weeks. So head into the great outdoors to make your own piece of "land art" using the materials you find in nature.

Once you start collecting things, you'll get a better idea of what you can make. Then start looking for the right location to make your masterpiece. Remember to take a picture of it when you're done because it won't last long! Oh yeah, and make sure you only use natural materials so you don't end up littering the landscape.

Andy Goldsworthy, *Beechleaves* (1999)

Pencils

Pencils are great. You can put them behind your ear, you can chew them, you can stick them in your hair and you can even draw with them! No matter what kind of super-awesome artist you want to be, one thing's for sure – you're going to be using loads of pencils. Most people think pencils are just pencils, but there are many different kinds of pencils and many different things you can do with them. It's time to sharpen up your skills with some essential pencil pointers.

Types of pencils

Pencils are either hard or soft. OK, there's also one that's kind of in the middle. More about those in a moment. Hard pencils are called H pencils and soft pencils are called B pencils. The marks you can make with pencils range from really light to really dark, depending on how hard or how soft a pencil is. See here:

B pencils

These pencils are great for doing sketches and shading because they make darker, thicker lines. The softer the pencil, the darker and thicker the line. Because these pencils are so soft, you'll need to keep sharpening them.

HB pencil

This pencil doesn't know if it's hard or soft, hence the name HB. This makes HB one of the most popular pencils because, when sharp, you can use it to make precise lines and, when blunter, you can use it for shading.

H pencils

These pencils are great for doing accurate drawings because they make thinner, lighter lines. Never press too hard with an H pencil because it can be so hard it will scratch into the paper.

Nifty know-how: shading

Shading is super-important because it adds depth and form to your drawing. It can transform a flat circle into a page-popping planet and turn simple doodles into three-dimensional shapes. Depending on what look you're going for, there are lots of different ways to shade your drawing.

Basic shading

By using the side of the pencil, you can create a soft, even patch of shading.

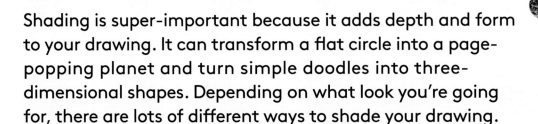

Smudging

Once you've laid down your basic shading, you can smudge it with your finger to create an even smoother patch of shading. It's hard to keep your smudging within the lines, but the great thing about smudging is that it's easy to tidy up with your eraser.

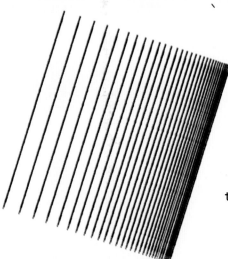

Hatching

Drawing parallel lines spaced apart creates an area of lighter shading, and drawing lines closer together creates an area of darker shading. You can create a "gradient" (smoothly changing from light to dark) by gradually making the lines closer together.

Cross-hatching

You can create even darker, more detailed shading by adding parallel lines on top of your hatching, at a 90-degree angle. And if you want, you can layer even more parallel lines on top of those.

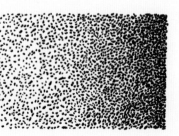

Stippling

Rather than drawing lines, you can make dots. The closer the dots, the darker the shading. You'll find that it's easier to "stipple" with softer pencils.

Nifty know-how: pencil tricks!

Because you're learning how to become a super-awesome artist, it's time to let you in on some secret tricks you can do with a pencil. But keep these to yourself, OK?

Holding your pencil

You probably already know the normal way to hold a pencil. It's like this:

But some super-awesome artists prefer to hold their pencil like this:

Because you're using the side of the pencil, it's a great technique to create really even shading.

Pivot your wrist

Don't move your forearm

Drawing a curve

When it comes to drawing perfect circles or curves, rest your forearm on the table to create stability and use the natural pivot of your wrist. Once you've drawn your curve, turn the paper around and continue.

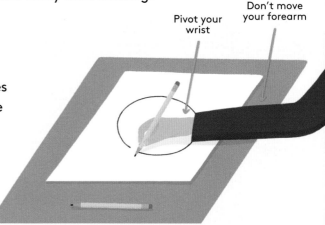

Slide forearm steadily along table

Drawing a straight line

When it comes to drawing straight lines, super-awesome artists rest their hand on the side of the table and run it up or down while holding the pencil on the paper.

Measuring stuff

Pencils are also great for measuring things so you can keep your drawings accurate and in proportion. By holding your arm fully outstretched, you can measure a subject to find out how wide something is in relation to its height.

By measuring this face with the pencil, you can see that it's twice as high as it is wide. Cool, eh?

Chuck Close, *Keith* (1970)

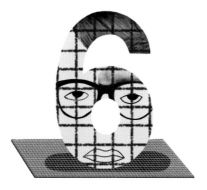

Obsess over detail

When you turned the page, I bet you instantly thought this was a photo, but you know what? It's actually a huge painting! The artist Chuck Close takes pictures of people and then copies them to create super-awesomely detailed drawings and paintings on a big scale. Making something this detailed and lifelike might seem impossible, but I'll let you into Chuck's secret. He draws a grid over the photo so the face is divided into small squares. Then he draws the same grid on his paper (only much bigger) and fills in each square one by one. This helps him focus on the details and keep the proportions exact. Try making your own super-detailed drawing or painting using Chuck's grid technique.

Your two grids can be different sizes, but it's essential – and I mean essential – that you keep the proportions of your grids the same. So, if your grid measures 10 squares by 20 squares on the photo, make sure it's the same on your paper.

Explore another dimension

Most of the time, people look at an artwork from only one angle – the front. But there's no "front" with sculptures. They are designed to be looked at and appreciated from all directions. It's kind of like making a million different artworks all in one! I love, and I mean LOVE, these sculptures by Rachel Beach. They stand taller than you and when you walk around them, the sharp angles and painted surfaces mean they are constantly changing. One minute they look like Native American totem poles and the next, futuristic skyscrapers or even robots! Cut up some boxes and glue them together to make your own large-scale sculpture that looks amazing from all angles.

It might help to sketch out your rough design first. Think about how the three-dimensional shapes and angles will work with the patterns and colours that you will eventually paint on your sculpture.

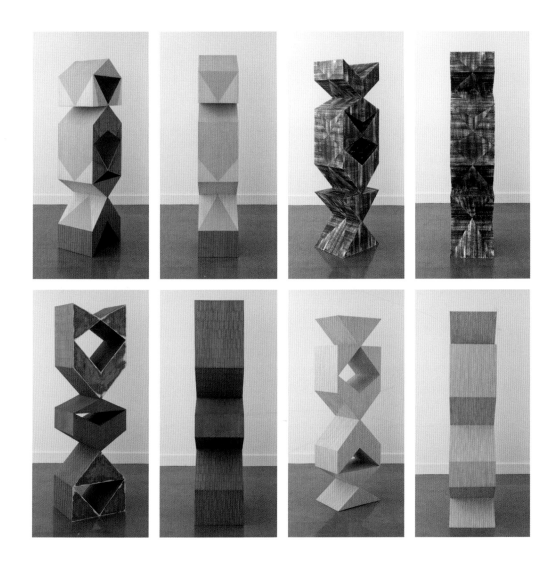

Rachel Beach, various views of her sculptures (2013)

John Stezaker, *Marriage* (2007–2008)

Combine and create

My friend John Stezaker likes to combine old photos of Hollywood film stars, and his creations are a little strange, to say the least! I love John's collages because he creates two pictures in one. You can still see both photos as individual people, but because the features fit together so perfectly, an entirely new face is created. It's as if John has made film-star monsters from two people who now exist as one! Collect photos from newspapers and magazines and have fun joining them together in interesting ways.

You don't have to make faces, like John. You could create weird landscapes, animals or objects. The main thing is to spot elements that make two different images fit together in surprising ways.

Be challenging

Who would've thought that one of the most significant artworks of the twentieth century wasn't an artwork at all. Not originally, anyway – it was a urinal! When the artist Marcel Duchamp placed his urinal in a gallery and gave it the name "Fountain", people cried out "This isn't art!" But when everyone calmed down, they started to think, "Well, if it's in a gallery, maybe it is art. And even though it's a urinal, it is kind of sculptural." With his bold act, Marcel forever changed what people perceived as "art". These kinds of artworks are called "ready-mades" because artists haven't really made or changed them. They just found something and exhibited it. Find your own ready-made to exhibit in your home. Give it a title that helps change how we perceive it and then defend its worthiness as "art" to your family and friends.

It's important to know why your ready-made is worthy of being a work of art. This challenge isn't just about being funny – it's about changing the way people relate to familiar objects. That's why the title you choose is so important.

Marcel Duchamp, *Fountain* (1950 version of 1914 original)

Aaron Johnson, *Dandy* (2013)

Be a scavenger

Aaron Johnson shows us that super-awesome art can be made out of anything – even socks! For this piece, Aaron glued socks to a board in the shape of a monster's face and then painted them in ghoulish green and other colours. The combination of materials – paint and socks – makes for a surprisingly fun and expressive picture. It's like the socks themselves are big, bold brushstrokes. For this challenge, use household items such as old clothes, food containers or whatever you can find to create your own artwork inspired by Aaron's.

Your picture could be of anything – such as a face, car, house or tree. Think about what colour you want the background to be, because you'll need to paint that before sticking stuff down.

Colour

Everyone has a favourite colour. But, in a way, it's weird to have one favourite colour because the impact and effect of colours change, depending on what colours are next to them. Colour is complicated like that, so here are some essential things you need to know.

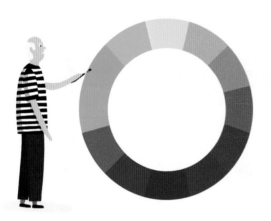

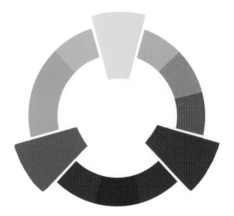

The colour wheel

The colour wheel helps artist like yourself make sense of colour. By grouping colours together, you can use the wheel to see which ones work together and why.

Primary colours

All the colours in the whole world start with just three: red, yellow, blue. They're called "primary" because all other colours are made by mixing them together in different ways.

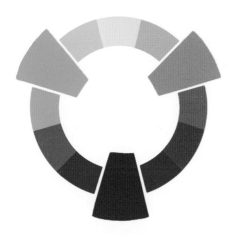

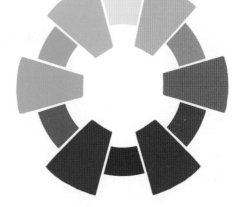

Secondary colours

Next, you have secondary colours: green, purple, orange. You make each of these by mixing two primary colours together. See how green sits between yellow and blue on the wheel? That's because you make green by mixing yellow and blue.

Tertiary colours

Now things get even more colourful (and complicated). To make a tertiary colour, you mix a primary colour with a secondary colour. See how mixing yellow (primary) and green (secondary) gives you lime (tertiary)?

Even super-awesome artists sometimes need to refer to the colour wheel when mixing paints. Keep this page handy or make your own super-awesome colour wheel.

Nifty know-how: colour

When placed next to each other, different colours create different effects. You can pick a palette of "harmonious colours" or "complementary colours". It's also important to understand that colours are emotional beings and each carries a different kind of mood.

Harmonious colours

Harmonious colours lie next to each other on the colour wheel and because they live next to each other, they all get along really well. Green and yellow, red and purple... See how easy on the eye these combinations are? They create a calm, harmonious effect.

Complementary colours

Complementary colours live opposite each other on the colour wheel and when they come together, you'd better stand back because they pop! See the effect when you place red and green next to each other, or purple and yellow? Rather than being calming, these combinations are full of energy.

The emotions of colours

The colours you choose to use in an artwork can affect the mood of the person looking at it. Depending on our personal experiences, the same colour could make different people feel different things. For example, I hate green because a big green monster once stole my lunch. But on the whole, we do generally respond to colour in the same ways. Here's a round-up of the emotions and qualities that various colours carry.

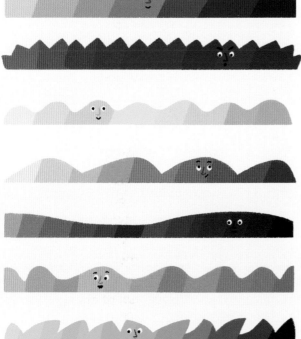

Blues: calm, peaceful, sad

Reds: anger, danger, passion

Yellows: friendly, happy, positive

Pinks: energetic, fun, pretty

Purples: luxurious, mature, serious

Oranges: enthusiastic, joyful, warm

Greens: fresh, natural, safe

Use colourful language

Lauren Badenhoop makes beautiful blobby paintings inspired by the colours of her home state of California. And when it comes to colour, California has it all, from blue skies and golden beaches to dusty deserts, lush green vineyards and massive mountains covered with bright white snow. Lauren carefully picks from the natural colours all around her to make harmonious, abstract paintings that reflect where she lives and how she feels. Make a blobby painting like Lauren's, inspired by the colours of where you live.

"Collect" colours by going on a walk and taking photos of the shades that catch your eye. When you get home, see which ones go together best and start mixing your paints to match the colours you've captured.

Lauren Badenhoop, *Dawn on Wade* (2020)

Frida Kahlo, *Self-portrait with Bonito* (1941)

Make it about you

Here's a self-portrait by the Mexican artist Frida Kahlo. Frida lived a life full of heartache and health problems, and often her self-portraits reflected how she was feeling. She painted this shortly after her dad died and it also features her parrot, Bonito, who had recently died too. Against a background of lush greenery, caterpillars and butterflies (which symbolise life and rebirth), Frida wears only black and is without any jewellery. She is clearly in mourning, and when she painted this she must have been missing her dad and Bonito very much. Paint your own self-portrait using props that reflect how you're feeling right now.

Self-portraits don't have to be about being sad. You might be really excited about something, such as your upcoming birthday or the school holidays. Think about your clothes, gather some props, and paint yourself in front of a mirror. If you can't find the props you need, simply use your imagination, like Frida!

Be a pop star

Roy Lichtenstein was called a "pop artist" because he made work based on popular culture, especially images from comic strips. Roy would find specific panels in comics and then turn them into huge paintings. What I love about Roy's painting is the fact that he completely removes the original story and focuses all our attention on the couple in the car. We have no idea where they are racing to and why, or if they are having fun or in the middle of an argument! Taking something out of its original setting, or "context", is super-fun because you can completely change its meaning. Start cutting out panels that become intriguing when removed from their original story in the comic and turn your favourites into stand-alone paintings.

Like Roy, you can change or simplify some parts of the original picture, depending on what you want your pop painting to look like. But when it comes to copying the main parts, you might find it helpful to use Chuck Close's grid technique (page 21).

Roy Lichtenstein, *In the Car* (1963)

René Magritte, *The Human Condition* (1933)

Make it strange

Maybe you've heard people use the word "surreal" before – like, "Last night I dreamed about a giant rainbow-coloured carrot that was being ridden by an elephant, wearing a top hat and tails. It was really surreal." René Magritte was known as a "surrealist" painter because when you look at his works, they make you start thinking strange things. Just look at this painting. It's like the painting in the painting is covering up the same view behind the painting in the painting, but how can there be any "painting" behind a painting in a painting because a painting is just a painting. For this challenge, create an impossible picture that makes people look at it and think "Huh...?"

Like René, you could use frames within frames. For example, someone could be looking in a mirror and everything could be reflected apart from them. Or it could be a landscape scene that combines day and night. Or you could paint mountains floating like clouds above the ocean... Anything goes!

Waste time

Who would have thought that white plastic milk bottles could be so beautiful!
Here, the artist Gayle Chong Kwan has glued together hundreds of empty
bottles so that they rise up and hang down like rock formations in an ancient
cave. Gayle's artwork makes you think about a disposable everyday object
in a totally new light and about the mountains of junk that end up polluting
the planet. Start rescuing plastic packaging from the bin to make your
own artwork. Turn your bedroom into a cave, make a towering skyscraper
or a humongous woolly mammoth! Just make sure it's so super-awesome
that no one will want to throw it away.

Plan what you're going to make in advance so you know what to collect.
You could collect the same piece of rubbish over time so your artwork
ends up being a single colour. Or you could combine plastic packaging
of different shapes, colours and sizes.

Gayle Chong Kwan, *Wastescape* (2012)

Paint

Paint is probably the most super-awesome art invention of all time. It comes in all kinds of different colours and consistencies, and is made up of all kinds of things – like water, oil and even plants! You can't be a super-awesome artist without knowing a thing or two about paint, so here goes...

Types of paint
There are three different types of paint:

Watercolours
Watercolours usually come in the form of little blocks of pigment or in tubes, but it's all the same stuff. To paint with watercolours, all you need to do is add water. A little water goes a long way and the more you add, the wishy-washier the paint becomes. Unlike other paints, watercolours are translucent, meaning they are semi-transparent.

Oils

Oils produce beautifully rich colours, and their thick consistency lends texture and depth to paintings. Unlike watercolours, oil paints are opaque, meaning you can completely cover things up when you paint on top of them. The downside of oil paints is that they take days and sometimes weeks to dry, so things take longer. Also, because their base ingredient is oil, this type of paint can't be dissolved in water, so you need to use something called turpentine to clean brushes.

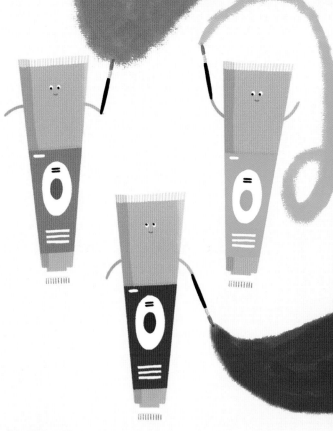

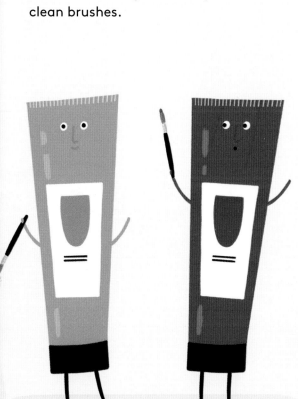

Acrylics

In painting terms, acrylics are the new kids on the block because they were invented only in the 1950s. Acrylics take the convenience of watercolour and the vividness of oils to create a versatile paint that is easy to control. Like oils, they are thick and opaque, but because they are water-based (like watercolours) they can be thinned or cleaned with water and they dry quickly. For young, super-awesome artists like yourself, acrylics are a great way to get started.

Nifty know-how: brushes 'n' stuff

Basically you have flat-head brushes, which are great for painting large areas, and round-head brushes, which are perfect for painting fine lines and details.

Brushes come in a range of sizes, from 000, which is super-small, all the way up to 30, which is really big. Picking the right brush depends on how big your painting is and how much detail it's going to contain, so it's good to have a range of shapes and sizes in your collection.

Keep it clean!
You'd be surprised how little paint you need on the end of your brush. Rather than plunge your brush into the paint, try to get into the habit of dipping it. And if you find that things are getting out of hand because there's too much paint on your brush, wash it all off, dry the brush and dip it again.

Other ways to paint

Brushes aren't the only things
super-awesome artists "paint" with.
Here are some other ways to create
interesting paint effects.

Palette knives

A palette knife is great if you want to put
down a lot of thick paint on your canvas, and
you can then spread it around like butter.
You can also use a palette knife to scratch
away at paint to create little highlights.

Sponges

Sponges are great for smudging
paint, dabbing on paint and creating
interesting textures. You can use
a big sponge for large areas, or tear
one up into small pieces to work
on fine details.

Vincent van Gogh, *Wheat Field with Cypresses* (1889)

Lay it on thick

You've probably heard of Vincent van Gogh. He's one of the most famous artists of all time. And with good reason. No matter the subject matter, his paintings were expressive and full of emotion. Look at how the sky and trees in this painting appear to swirl around, as if being blown about by the wind. To create this effect, Vincent used a painting technique called "impasto", which means he laid on the paint really thick to create big, bold marks. Light also reflects off impasto paintings in interesting ways because the surface is uneven, rather than flat. Try making your own equally expressive impasto painting.

Many artists who use the impasto technique will apply the paint with a palette knife, rather than a brush, a little like someone slopping on cement while laying a brick wall. Use acrylics or oil paints, as they're much thicker than watercolours.

Play up

Tehching Hsieh is a "performance artist", which means he creates artwork out of the things he does, or acts out, in real life. These photos are a record of one of his works called *Art Life/One Year Performance (Rope Piece)*. Get this: for *Rope Piece*, Tehching tied himself to his friend and fellow artist, Linda Montano, for one whole year! Tehching and Linda had to do everything together and as you can imagine, that wasn't so easy after a while. Although it's a funny idea, *Rope Piece* is actually quite a serious artwork because it makes us reflect on the privilege of freedom, the need for human connection and the importance of tolerance. Think about what's important to you – perhaps you want to raise awareness about the homeless or climate change – and then make your own piece of performance art inspired by that. Oh, and you don't have to do something for a whole year. It's OK if your performance lasts just a few minutes.

You can be silly or serious when making your own piece of performance art, just as long as there's a point or greater meaning to what you are doing. Don't forget to document your performance, either with photos or videos, because I'd love to see what you do. Post your performance online using #BeSuperAwesome.

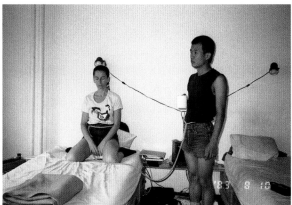

Tehching Hsieh, *Art Life/One Year Performance (Rope Piece)* (1983–1984)

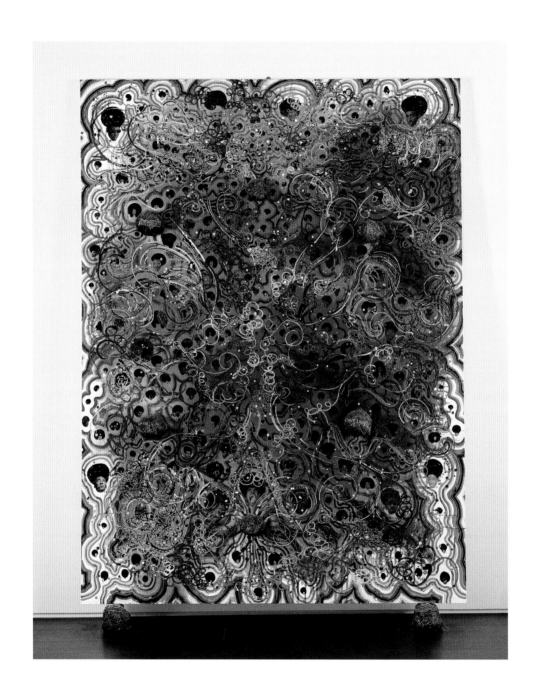

Chris Ofili, *Afrodizzia (Second version)* (1996)

Tell us who you are

Chris Ofili makes work using elephant dung. Yes, you read that right. He takes nice big round pieces of poop and sticks them on to his canvases along with visually vibrant materials like glitter, paint, resin and magazine cut-outs. Chris is a British person with Nigerian parents, and his art explores his rich and diverse cultural history that includes aspects of Africa and the UK. In this picture, he has included references to people of colour, as well as the names of significant sports stars and musicians, such as Cassius Clay (aka Muhammad Ali) and Miles Davis. Wondering why elephant dung? Keep up! Where do elephants live? By using unexpected materials, Chris is using his artistic freedom to play with the mix of cultural references and stereotypes that are present in his work. For this challenge, I want you to make an artwork inspired by your own cultural history. It can be a simple painting or you could incorporate materials that are relevant to your ancestry.

No matter the colour of your skin, your religious beliefs or your nationality, you have a cultural history. Perhaps your parents or grandparents aren't originally from where you live now. Perhaps you are a unique combination of two or more different races, regions or religions. One thing's for sure, you're not 100 per cent anything!

Celebrate what you love

Yayoi Kusama loves, and I mean loves, pumpkins. It's not necessarily because of their taste, more so because of all the vivid memories Yayoi has of this blobby fruit growing in the fields surrounding her childhood home. They were all so unique and strange-looking. Now, Yayoi paints pictures of pumpkins, sculpts giant pumpkins and sometimes even makes her pumpkins light up in the dark. To experience her art is a little like stepping into her childhood mind! I bet there's something you love as much as Yayoi loves pumpkins. Perhaps it's a food, object, person or pet. Whatever it is, make lots of lovely art inspired by your something...

Figuring out why you love your something is important because your artwork needs to celebrate that quality. See how Yayoi has made pumpkins even more funny-looking by exaggerating their shape and covering them with dots.

Yayoi Kusama, *All the Eternal Love I Have for the Pumpkins* (2016)

Clockwise from top left: Joan Miró, Frida Kahlo, Pablo Picasso, Angelica Kauffman, Albrecht Dürer, Gustav Klimt, Henri de Toulouse-Lautrec, Vincent van Gogh, Paul Cézanne and Leonardo da Vinci

Make your mark

Every super-awesome artist needs a super-awesome signature. Some artists, like Angelica Kauffman, chose to sign their whole name. Others, like Vincent van Gogh, signed only their first name. (I mean, how many "Vincents" do you know?) Lucky people with really cool names, like Pablo Picasso, signed only their last names. And artists like Albrecht Dürer made an icon using his initials, AD. For this final challenge, create your own super-awesome artist's signature that you can put on all your artworks from now on. That way, everyone will know it was made by you and is worth a bazillion gazillion dollars!

Traditionally, artists sign their pictures on the bottom right. But you don't have to. Some artists also like to hide their signatures somewhere in their paintings!

A brief history of art

6000–30 BCE

Prehistoric paintings

It's not possible to say exactly when "art" started, but some of the oldest surviving works were made over 40,000 years ago. They were painted on the walls of caves by our human ancestors, the Neanderthals. These cave paintings mostly depicted animals, and the paints were made out of ground-up rocks and plants.

Ancient Egyptian art

People made art all over the world and because cultures were so unique and disconnected, the results all looked very different. Perhaps the most famous early artists were the ancient Egyptians. These guys would make giant stone carvings of their kings and queens (pharaohs) and fill tombs with paintings and sculptures to help people in the afterlife. I suppose you could say the ancient Egyptians were the world's most committed artists, because rather than write words, they wrote with pictures called "hieroglyphs".

500 BCE – 400 CE

Classical art

Western art (that's art made in Europe and later the Americas) really kicked off with the Greeks and Romans. They would carve realistic sculptures of mythological figures out of marble and paint bowls, pots and plates to tell stories about their gods.

400–1450

Medieval art

Nothing lasts forever, and after the Romans conquered the Greeks and northern Europeans later conquered the Romans, the classical civilization ended. This ushered in a new era of art, and mega amounts of it were produced during this period. Funded by the Christian Church, much of it featured saints and illustrated stories from the Bible. No expense was spared... Often it was even made with gold and jewels!

A brief history of art

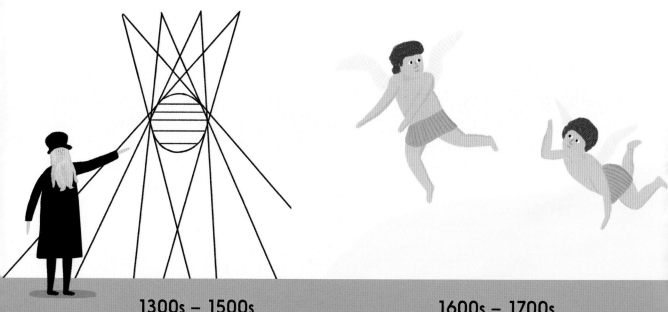

1300s – 1500s

Renaissance art

Renaissance, meaning "rebirth", looked back to classical art for inspiration and depicted more fantastical scenes that looked like they were set within the real world. Perhaps the most significant thing about Renaissance art was the invention of "perspective". Perspective is a painting and drawing technique that creates the illusion of depth, or three-dimensional space, on a flat surface. We take perspective for granted now, but back then it was revolutionary! One of the most celebrated renaissance artists was Leonardo da Vinci.

1600s – 1700s

Baroque art

Baroque (pronounced "buh-rok") took the traditions of Renaissance art and ramped it up even more. Artists still made paintings about gods, myths and Christianity but gave everything a more theatrical twist. The lighting became more dramatic, the scenes more epic, and much less emphasis was placed on depicting reality as it was. Want to paint the Virgin Mary, flying through the sky? No problem. Throw in a couple of cherubs too!

1750 – 1850

Neoclassic and Romantic art

Neoclassicism and Romanticism were two different art movements that occurred at the same time, but both had very different ideas and themes. Neoclassic artists tended to create formal compositions with moral messages. Meanwhile, the work of Romantic artists was more imaginative and emotional. Believe it or not, before 1800, landscapes were used only as backgrounds for other things, but now they finally took centre stage and became the subject of paintings in their own right.

1860s – 1900s

Impressionism, Post-impressionism, Expressionism

This is when things started to get modern. Impressionism and then Post-impressionism (post meaning "after") broke away from age-old styles, rules and subjects. Paintings became smaller because many were made outside (also referred to as "en plein air", which is French for "outside"). And their subject matter focused on everyday places rather than gods and myths. This period of art was all about colour and emotion, especially later, when the Expressionists got going.

1907 – 1914

Abstract art
Abstract art was the most significant movement in Western art since the Renaissance. Now artists were challenging everything. Rules and traditions where torn up, even perspective, and making things look even slightly realistic was no longer considered cool. Maybe you've heard of Pablo Picasso? He was one of the most famous artists of this period.

1950s – 1970s

Pop art
Pop artists didn't want to make big splatty abstract paintings. Instead they wanted to make things referencing the stuff they saw and used every day. Often pop artists would copy brand names, food packaging and comics strips, but make them way bigger so familiar things became more meaningful.

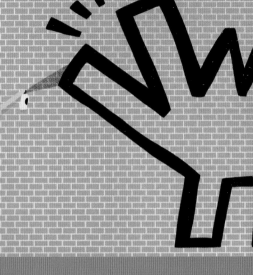

1977 – present day

1980s – present day

Contemporary art

These days artists have the freedom to do pretty much whatever they want using whatever they want! The lines between painting, sculpture, photography and film have become blurred because contemporary artists often like to mash things up. It's an exciting time for art, because artists are making work about everything and anything, and massive museums put on blockbuster shows that attract millions of people.

Street art

People have been painting graffiti for thousands of years. Even cave paintings are a kind of graffiti. But it wasn't until the 1980s that graffiti started to get taken seriously and people referred to it as "street art". Often street art carries a political or social message and because it's seen everywhere, rather than just in galleries, it reaches and influences a lot of people.

Published by
Laurence King Publishing Ltd
361–373 City Road
London EC1V 1LR
United Kingdom
T + 44 (0)20 7841 6900
enquiries@laurenceking.com
www.laurenceking.com

© Text 2020 Henry Carroll

A catalogue record for this book
is available from the British Library.

ISBN: 978-1-78627-762-6

Commissioning editor: Jo Lightfoot
Editor: Charlotte Selby
Designer: Katerina Kerouli
Picture researcher: Peter Kent
Production: Davina Cheung

Printed in Italy

Laurence King Publishing is committed to
ethical and sustainable production. We are
proud participants in The Book Chain Project®
bookchainproject.com

Picture credits

5: © Succession Picasso/DACS, London 2020. Photo ©RMN-Grand Palais (Musée national Picasso-Paris)/Adrien Didierjean; 6: *Convergence*, 1952. Oil on canvas, framed: 241.935 x 399.0975 x 7.3025 cm (95¼ x 157⅛ x 2⅞ in); Gift of Seymour H. Knox, Jr., 1956. Albright Knox Art Gallery/Art Resource, NY/Scala, Florence. © The Pollock-Krasner Foundation ARS, NY and DACS, London 2020; 9: Lorna Simpson, All images: Collage and ink on paper. 28.6 x 21.6 cm (11¼ x 8½ in) TL Blue Light, 2012. (Inv# LS 2018.unique). TC At Large, 2012. (Inv# LS 2021.unique). TR Big Yellow, 2011. (Inv# LS 1947.unique). CL Black Cloud, 2011. (Inv# LS 1951.unique). CC Before Enlistment, 2011. (Inv# LS 1959. unique). CR Day Before, 2012. (Inv# LS 2025.unique). BL Blue, 2011. (Inv# LS 1952.unique). BC Blue Fro, 2011. (Inv# LS 1957. unique). BR Blue Wave, 2011. (Inv# LS 1949.unique); 10: *Straight Curve*, 1963. Emulsion on board. 71.1 x 62.2 cm. © Bridget Riley 2019. All rights reserved. Courtesy Bridget Riley Archive; 13: Beech leaves laid over a pool. Rained overnight. River rose. Washing the leaves downstream. Scaur Water, Dumfriesshire. 30 October 1999. © Andy Goldsworthy; 20: Keith, 1970. Saint Louis Art Museum. 275 x 213.4 cm (108¼ x 84 in). Funds given by the Shoenberg Foundation, Inc. Object Number 793:1983. © Chuck Close, courtesy Pace Gallery; 23: Rachel Beach TL, TCL Buttress, TCR, TR Link, BL, BCL Tink, BCR, BR Husk, 2013. Photos: Cary Whittier; 24: John Stezaker TL Marriage (Film Portrait Collage) L, 2008 Collage 27 x 18 cm (10⅝ x 7⅛ in) AP-STEZJ-00577. TR Marriage (Film Portrait Collage) XLV, 2007 Collage 25.5 x 20.5 cm (10 x 8⅛ in) AP-STEZJ-00506. BL Marriage (Film Portrait Collage) XXV, 2007 Collage 27.5 x 20.5 cm (10⅞ x 8⅛ in) AP-STEZJ-00443. BR Marriage (Film Portrait Collage) XXXII, 2007 Collage 24.8 x 18.5 cm (9¾ x 7¼ in) AP-STEZJ-00487. © Approach Gallery, London; 27: *Fountain*, 1950 version of 1914 original, Philadelphia Museum of Art. © Association Marcel Duchamp/ADAGP, Paris and DACS, London 2020; 28: *Dandy*, 2013, acrylic and socks on linen, 51 x 41 cm (20 x 16 in), 2013. Image courtesy and © Aaron Johnson; 35: Image courtesy and © Lauren Badenhoop; 36: *Self-portrait with Bonito*, 1941. Oil on canvas. Height: 55 cm (21.65 in), Width: 43.4 cm (17.09 in) Private collection/Alamy. © Banco de México Diego Rivera Frida Kahlo Museums Trust, Mexico, D.F./DACS 2020; 39: akg-images/Album/Fine Art Images. © Estate of Roy Lichtenstein/DACS 2020; 40: National Gallery of Art. Washington DC. Photothèque R. Magritte/Adagp Images, Paris/Scala, Florence. © ADAGP, Paris and DACS, London 2020; 43: *Wastescape*, Southbank Centre, London. 2012 Installation, used plastic milk bottles and sound works. Variable size. © Gayle Chong Kwan; 48: Metropolitan Museum of Art, New York. Purchase, The Annenberg Foundation Gift, 1993. 1993.132 (Open Access); 51: © Tehching Hsieh and Linda Montano. Courtesy the artists and Sean Kelly Gallery, New York; 52: *Afrodizzia (Second version)*, signed, titled and dated 1996 on the stretcher, acrylic, oil, polyester resin, paper collage, glitter, map pins and elephant dung on linen canvas: 243.8 x 182.8 cm (95¹⁵⁄₁₆ x 71¹⁵⁄₁₆ in), overall: 252.1 x 182.9 cm (99¼ x 71¹⁵⁄₁₆ in). Courtesy of the artist and Victoria Miro Gallery; 55: Yayoi Kusama, *All the Eternal Love I Have for the Pumpkins*, 2016; Wood, mirror, plastic, acrylic and LED, 292.4 x 415 x 415 cm (115 ⅛ x 163⅜ x 163⅜ in). Courtesy the artist, Ota Fine Arts and Victoria Miro. © Yayoi Kusama.

Thanks!

This book would not have been possible without the help of Charlotte Selby, Laurence King, Jo Lightfoot, Peter Kent, Rose Blake, Katerina Kerouli, Katherine Cowles and Selwyn Leamy. And a big final thank you goes to all the super-awesome artists who kindly agreed to have their work featured in this book.

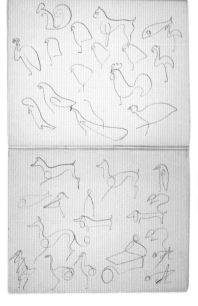

Pablo Picasso, 'Dachshund/Sausage Dog', detail in pen and Indian ink on beige paper from a sketchbook Zervos VI n°972 (1907)